This journal belongs to

_____

_____

_____

_____

E.M. Williams Publishing
Baltimore, Maryland

Copyright © 2024 Dr. Jasmine L. Leigh Morse

All rights reserved. No portion of this book may be reproduced without permission in writing from the publisher, except in the case of brief quotations in reviews.

DISCLAIMER

This book is for entertainment purposes only. It is not intended to substitute for medical advice, counseling, or treatment. Any person with a condition requiring medical attention should consult a qualified medical professional. The information in this book is not meant to be taken as expert advice. The views expressed in this book are those of the author alone and should not be considered instructional or authoritative.

Neither the author nor the publisher assumes any responsibility or liability whatsoever on behalf of the purchaser or reader of these materials. Neither the author nor the publisher assumes any responsibility or liability for any loss, damage, disruption, or contrary interpretations of the subject matter therein. Neither the author nor the publisher is responsible for or liable for any adverse effects resulting from the use of the suggestions outlined in this book.

All Scripture quotations, unless otherwise indicated, are taken from the Holy Bible, New International Version®, NIV®. Copyright ©1973, 1978, 1984, 2011 by Biblica, Inc.™ Used by permission of Zondervan. All rights reserved worldwide. www.zondervan. comThe "NIV" and "New International Version" are trademarks registered in the United States Patent and Trademark Office by Biblica, Inc.™

Scripture quotations from The Authorized (King James) Version. Rights in the Authorized Version in the United Kingdom are vested in the Crown. Reproduced by permission of the Crown's patentee, Cambridge University Press

Scripture taken from the New King James Version®. Copyright © 1982 by Thomas Nelson. Used by permission. All rights reserved.

Hardcover ISBN: 978-1-7358080-5-5
Paperback ISBN: 978-1-7358080-4-8

For information about the Girl Go Global™ community or the author, speaker requests, or media inquiries, please visit www.girlgoglobal.com or email hello@girlgoglobal.com.
Or, connect with the author on social media:

Instagram: @drjasmineleighmorse or @girlgoglobal_
Facebook: Dr. Jasmine Leigh Morse or Girl Go Global™
LinkedIn: Jasmine Leigh Morse, PhD

A DEVOTIONAL JOURNAL
—— FOR ——
DISCOVERING, EMBRACING, AND IGNITING YOUR PURPOSE

DR. JASMINE LEIGH MORSE
E.M. WILLIAMS PUBLISHING
BALTIMORE

Hey Global Girl!

Do you know that your purpose is calling you? And I believe you have encountered this devotional journal because the Lord wants you to discover, embrace, and ignite your purpose.

Whether your purpose is something you have always known, you are continuously working toward, or have yet to embrace, I believe living in purpose is one of the most powerful things you can seek to do. I also believe that purpose needs to be explored and understood. And, as we explore the depths of our purpose, I believe we realize that purpose evolves, grows, and calls us to do more . . . and more . . . and more in service of it. Most of all, I believe we should seek to understand God's purpose for our lives; otherwise, we are simply making plans. I think Proverbs 19:21 says it best: *"Many are the plans in a person's heart, but it is the Lord's purpose that prevails."* Here, Proverbs reveals the necessity for seeking our God-given purpose. It also acknowledges the duality between a life mired by our own plans and one lived beyond our human potential.

So, here I am with my own call to help other women reach destiny and purpose. I have felt beckoned to unpack tactical methods and strategies for discovering, embracing, and igniting purpose. While some of us are fortunate enough to know exactly what we want to be when we grow up, I know there are those who need a little more time and support to discover their God-given path to purpose. Likewise, I created the *Girl Go Global*™ devotional journal for women who need clarity about their purpose and for women who are seeking continuous evolution. This journal is not only a call to action; it is designed to help women, like you, embrace their multi-layered lives. Overall,

I aim to empower you to join your faith and your works, in order to live the courageous life for which God created you. In doing so, I aim to help you embrace the calling you feel from within, step into your power, and fulfill your true destiny and purpose in life.

So, let's go global and embrace our multi-layered lives with faith, know-how, and grit.

XOXO,

Dr. Jasmine

What does it mean for girls to go global?

Girl Go Global™ is not only a call to action but a community for women. It is designed to empower women to join their faith and their works in order to live the courageous life for which God created them. For the woman who is ready to embrace the calling that she feels from within, step into her power, and fulfill her true destiny and purpose in life, Dr. Jasmine created *Girl Go Global*™. This journal is, therefore, an accompaniment to the resources provided to women through the *Girl Go Global*™ network and community.

What does it mean to find your purpose?

To have clarity regarding why you were created.

How to use this journal

Whenever you set aside time to explore the pages of this journal, I encourage you to begin with prayer and by reciting the *Girl Go Global*™ Purpose Declaration:

> *My purpose fuels me with the audacity to save lives, empower, teach, and equip others for the glory of God.*

This journal aims to help you unpack the depths of your purpose, even if it is something you have always known, are working toward, or have yet to understand. Likewise, the *Girl Go Global*™ devotional journal is divided into three sections:

- Discovering Purpose
- Embracing Purpose
- Igniting Purpose

So, whether you explore these pages in 30, 90, or 365 days, allow time, space, and grace for the Lord to give you the answers you need for your future. Likewise, each of these sections are designed to offer you faith-based, tactical methods and strategies for examining or reexamining the layers of your purpose. Not only that, this journal will help you set the stage for thinking about and focusing on living a purpose-filled life. Included in each section are:

- Inspirational Quotes,
- Devotional Readings & Prayers,
- Study Scriptures,
- Writing Prompts,
- Exercises, and
- Creative, Freewrite Space.

You are free to discover, embrace, and ignite your purpose at your own pace. Wherever you find yourself in your journey, couple your faith with intentional, focused action.

Contents

Path to Purpose Self-Assessment   **10**

DISCOVERING PURPOSE

Clarity of Purpose	15
Realizing Your Strengths	31
Understanding Your Value	45

EMBRACING PURPOSE

Identifying Your Purpose	63
Living Out Your Vision & Mission	77
Setting Purpose-Filled Goals	89

IGNITING PURPOSE

Creating a Purpose-Filled Plan	105
Tracking the Success of Your Purpose-Filled Plan	119
Re-evaluating Your Ever-Evolving Purpose-Filled Plan	136
Purpose Notes	147

About The Author   **200**

Path to Purpose Self-Assessment

Answer the following questions to help you start generating ideas and thoughts about your purpose.

What are your top five goals in life?

What do you value most about who you are?

What makes you look forward to getting up in the morning?

What do you need the most every day?

What motivates you?

What inspires you?

Which one of your many skills stands out most to you?

Your talents run deep. Which of them could the world benefit from?

What are the top three things people should know about you?

Discovering Purpose

A life surrendered to the Lord will lead you
to discover your God-given purpose.

Through self-discovery, the Lord gives us the capacity to construct and frame a powerful existence for His Glory.

Clarity of Purpose

Trust in the LORD with all your heart and lean not on your own understanding; in all your ways submit to him, and he will make your paths straight.
(Proverbs 3:5-6)

Have you ever really paused to think about how unique you are? I mean, really paused to recognize that God customized your identity for the time you are living in right now. Do you realize that there is someone out there who needs you and what you possess? Not only that, did you know that you were created to create?

Of the millions of people around the world, it is pretty mind-blowing to know that each of us has our own fingerprint, footprint, and imprint. Our individual uniqueness is the distinguishing mark that shapes who we are and gives us our identity and creativity. Yet, though we are all one-of-a-kind, we were all created by God and given the same purpose-filled instruction from the beginning of creation, as described in Genesis 1:26-27,

> *Then God said, "Let us make mankind in our image, in our likeness, so that they may rule over the fish in the sea and the birds in the sky, over the livestock and all the wild animals, and over all the creatures that move along the ground." So God created mankind in his own image, in the image of God he created them; male and female he created them.*

As an image of God, our likeness of Him is less about His physical appearance and more about how we embody His attributes, much like what Psalm 145:8 says, *"The Lord is gracious and compassionate, slow to anger and rich in love."* I love how Galatians 5:22-26 expounds on how we should live a life in the likeness of God. Here, the Apostle Paul shares with us the characteristics of God by describing the fruit of the Spirit.

> *But the fruit of the Spirit is love, joy, peace, forbearance, kindness, goodness, faithfulness, gentleness and self-control. Against such things there is no law. Those who belong to Christ Jesus have crucified the flesh with its passions and desires. Since we live by the Spirit, let us keep in step with the Spirit. Let us not become conceited, provoking and envying each other.*

As we yield ourselves to a relationship with God and subsequently His Spirit, Paul is ultimately sharing the prescription for living as an image of God. As such, we will have no choice but to exhibit the attributes of God on the Earth.

So, when I circle back to God's instruction in Genesis 1:26-27, "*. . . Let us make mankind in our image, in our likeness,*" I have clarity about purpose, as this Scripture speaks to our collective purpose on Earth. First, I recognize that we have the capacity to be in a relationship with God. As our relationship with Him grows, we will have no choice but to become more like Him. Once we begin to reflect His likeness, it is one of our jobs to join with the Father to make mankind in His image. Likewise, I feel the weight and the responsibility to help others recognize how they can become more like our Heavenly Father. In doing so, the second element of purpose rests in the notion that I, like my Heavenly Father, have the ability to create. Just as He created me, I have the capacity to help Him create and walk people through the journey of developing a relationship with Him.

So, clarity of purpose comes when we understand and embody the true nature of the Lord in ways that we become more like Him, as His fruit in the Earth. Likewise, we will begin to resemble and replicate the Lord's grace, compassion, and love, along with the fruit of the Spirit. Then, we will echo what Apostle Paul means when he explains that our lives are not our own. Once we lean into a deeper relationship with the Lord, He will begin to point us toward the skills, abilities, gifts, and talents that He wants us to use to save lives, empower, teach, train, and equip others for His glory.

Dear Heavenly Father,

You knew me before I was formed in my mother's womb. Lord, You alone know why You created me. You alone understand my purpose here on Earth. You alone can forgive me for the times when I walked in my own way. Today, I surrender my life to Your perfect will and plan for my life. I surrender my life to a deeper relationship with You that I may embrace with clarity the desire to embrace Your attributes, Your image, and Your likeness. Father, as I become more and more like You, I want to thank You in advance for giving me clarity regarding why I was born and for who I was born to help, empower, teach, train, and equip for Your glory. Lord, thank You for the desire to surrender to Your purpose for my life. Thank You for giving me so many skills, abilities, and talents to use to build Your Kingdom.

In Jesus' name I pray. Amen.

Discovering Purpose Study Scriptures

May these scriptures lead you to discover or further explore your purpose. Read, study, or meditate on them day, night, or anytime in between.

Trust in the Lord with all your heart and lean not on your own understanding; in all your ways submit to him, and he will make your paths straight. (Proverbs 3:5-6)

But the fruit of the Spirit is love, joy, peace, forbearance, kindness, goodness, faithfulness, gentleness and self-control. Against such things there is no law. Those who belong to Christ Jesus have crucified the flesh with its passions and desires. Since we live by the Spirit, let us keep in step with the Spirit. Let us not become conceited, provoking and envying each other. (Galatians 5:23-26)

Date: ___ / ___ / ___

What daily, weekly, or monthly activities do you perform that bring you the greatest joy? Be sure to explain how and why.

Date: ___ / ___ / ___

What are your core values and how do they shape how you show up in the world?

Date: ___ / ___ / ___

If you had an opportunity to step into your future and replay your life, what legacy did you leave in the world?

Purpose & Passion

How do you define purpose and passion in your life? Can they coexist, or does one take precedence over the other?

_____
_____
_____
_____
_____
_____
_____
_____

Write down your top passions in life. Then, use the next few days, weeks, or months to pray and seek the Lord regarding which of those passions is something He wants you to pursue as part of your purpose right now. Remember, purpose is not one-note; it evolves and grows, and the depth of your purpose is meant to be explored. Now, start with the passions you have right now.

I am passionate about . . .

1. _____
2. _____
3. _____
4. _____
5. _____
6. _____
7. _____

8. _____
9. _____
10. _____

Hey Global Girl,
You were created to create!

Here is space to write, create, or do both.

Date: ___ / ___ / ___

Date: ___ / ___ / ___

How heroic and powerful it can be to construct an identity that draws inspiration, strength, and purpose out of crisis and chaos for God's glory.

Realizing Your Strengths

At moments of crisis and chaos, that is when I began to realize my creativity, adaptation skills, and strength. In my lowest and weakest moments, I realize my resilience and ability to learn and grow through stifling circumstances. Most of all, these moments have helped me understand my truest self and, ultimately, my greatest strengths.

I have felt the kind of pressure and hardship that left me weeping and pleading to God for help on my bedroom floor. Now, looking back, I realize hardships are momentary challenges that can either make or break you. Likewise, it is our job to lean into the full knowledge of Romans 5:3-5,

> *Not only so, but we also glory in our sufferings, because we know that suffering produces perseverance; perseverance, character; and character, hope. And hope does not put us to shame, because God's love has been poured out into our hearts through the Holy Spirit, who has been given to us.*

I love how this Scripture lets us know that if we lean into our faith and find hope and peace in God, we will be able to overcome challenges. More importantly, we will wake up on the other side of challenges with value added to our identity in ways that leave us better than we were. Woven within the perseverance, character, and hope that Romans talks about . . . if we search deep enough, we will find signs of a purpose that is often birthed out of suffering.

Therein, we find the capacity to pinpoint our greatest strengths, which often lead to a life lived on purpose if we let it. What a glorious moment it is to celebrate a state of overcoming by recognizing what God has placed on the inside of us for His glory, as Romans 8:18 states, *"I consider that our present sufferings are not worth comparing with the glory that will be revealed in us."*

For me, Romans 5:3-5 lets us know that as we continue to push through life's hardships, our character and identity will be shaped into something that honors the Lord and mirrors His likeness. And that new, redefined hope will produce an undeniable persistence and faith that allows us to show up in the world with all our greatest strengths shining in ways that give God glory.

Father,

I recognize You as Lord over my life. You are a God of love and compassion, and You are also a God that gives instruction and correction. I surrender to Your perfect will and plan for my life. Father, grant me the wisdom to follow Your ways and align with what You have for me to do. I look to You for the help I need to understand myself and my purpose. I look to You for ways to use my skills, talents, and abilities to make a positive impact in the world. And, as I point people back to You through my purpose, I thank You in advance for the people who will see Your image and likeness in me.

In Jesus' name. Amen.

Discovering Purpose Study Scriptures

May these scriptures lead you to discover or further explore your purpose. Read, study, or meditate on them day, night, or anytime in between.

I praise you because I am fearfully and wonderfully made; your works are wonderful, I know that full well. (Psalm 139:14)

For we are God's handiwork, created in Christ Jesus to do good works, which God prepared in advance for us to do. (Ephesians 2:10)

"Again, it will be like a man going on a journey, who called his servants and entrusted his wealth to them. To one he gave five bags of gold, to another two bags, and to another one bag, each according to his ability. Then he went on his journey. The man who had received five bags of gold went at once and put his money to work and gained five bags more. So also, the one with two bags of gold gained two more. But the man who had received one bag went off, dug a hole in the ground and hid his master's money. (Matthew 25:14-18)

Continue reading The Parable of the Bags of Gold in your favorite study Bible.

Date: ___ / ___ / ___

Imagine a conversation between you and a mentor, trusted advisor, or someone who knows you best. In what ways could they help you identify your strengths?

Date: ___ / ___ / ___

Reflect on a time when you felt confident in your abilities. What strengths were you drawing on, and what were you doing?

_____
_____
_____
_____
_____
_____
_____
_____
_____
_____
_____
_____
_____
_____
_____
_____
_____
_____
_____
_____

Date: ___ / ___ / ___

Think of a challenge you overcame. What strengths did you rely on to navigate through it?

_____
_____
_____
_____
_____
_____
_____
_____
_____
_____
_____
_____
_____
_____
_____
_____
_____
_____
_____
_____
_____
_____
_____
_____

List your top five to ten strengths. Think about anything from preparing chef-quality meals, and organizing people to strong public speaking abilities. Then, think about how those strengths can positively serve and support others.

My Top Strengths	Strategy for Serving and Supporting Others

Hey Global Girl,
Your purpose is calling you to make use of all your skills, talents, and abilities!

Here is space to write, create, or do both.

Date: ___ / ___ / ___

Date: ___ / ___ / ___

Discovering your God-given purpose should provoke an identity transformation that becomes so compelling and recognizable that people have no choice but to acknowledge the value you add to their lives.

Understanding Your Value

Ever had one of those days when you felt small, insignificant, or unclear about the value you have to add to others? Have you ever felt like you are just another face in the crowd who is easily overlooked and forgotten? If you find yourself saying yes to any of these questions, you are not alone. I, too, have felt some of these feelings and emotions. Yet, although these feelings and emotions are very real, we must recognize that Satan sends lies and deception to make us feel worthless and invaluable. He wants to keep us from recognizing the value God placed on the inside of us.

But today, I want to remind you that God sees you. He sees every tear you have shed, every smile you have shared, and every struggle you have faced. And, guess what? He cares about every detail of your life. Matter-of-fact, the Lord loves you so much that He created you. He wants to partner with you to create something that will make His name great in the Earth. He trusts and believes in who you are so much, so that He gave you dominion in the Earth as described in Genesis 1:26.

Global Girl, there is a version of you that God wants to reveal to you. But first, I encourage you to get to know how valuable you are to Him. Once you begin to understand your value in God, you will awaken to the value you have to add to the world around you. Matthew 10:29-31 helps God's care and concern for us come alive. Jesus uses a simple example to show us just how much He cares about us. Matthew speaks about the sparrow, a tiny bird that is seen through our human understanding as worthless. The Bible says two sparrows were worth no more than a penny. And yet, not a single one of them falls to the ground without God noticing.

If God cares that much about sparrows, how much more does He care about you? How much more does He recognize and see you? *Global Girl*, you came from God—the God who created the universe and all things in it. You are not just a random blip on the radar; you are a masterpiece that is intricately crafted by the hands of The Almighty. Your worth does not come from what you do or how you look; it comes from being a beloved child of God.

So, when you start to doubt your value, remember who you are and who you came from. You are worth more than many sparrows—loved, valued, and cherished by your Heavenly Father.

Lord,

I do not have elaborate words today. Some days, it is hard to remember my own worth in a world that is constantly telling me I am not enough. But Your Word reminds me that I am fearfully and wonderfully made, valued, and cherished by You.
Help me to see myself through Your eyes, as Your beloved child. Let Your love and acceptance be the foundation of my identity, and may I live each day knowing that I am deeply loved and valued by You. May I live each day knowing that I was born for a reason and a purpose. Help me to understand my why and reveal my how.

In Jesus' name I pray. Amen.

Discovering Purpose Study Scriptures

May these scriptures lead you to discover or further explore your purpose. Read, study, or meditate on them day, night, or anytime in between.

You are the light of the world. A town built on a hill cannot be hidden. (Matthew 5:14)

"But you are a chosen race, a royal priesthood, a holy nation, a people for his own possession, that you may proclaim the excellencies of him who called you out of darkness into his marvelous light." (1 Peter 2:9)

Date: ___ / ___ / ___

Reflect on a time when someone expressed gratitude and thanks for your help. Explore what you did, and how it made you feel? How does this experience reveal your unique value?

_____
_____
_____
_____
_____
_____
_____
_____
_____
_____
_____
_____
_____
_____
_____
_____
_____
_____
_____
_____
_____
_____
_____
_____

Date: ___ / ___ / ___

What skills, talents, or abilities come natural to you? In what ways have these abilities positively impacted your life or the lives of others?

Date: ___ / ___ / ___

Reflect on the feedback you receive from friends, family, or colleagues. What compliments or acknowledgments do you receive often? How do these affirm your worth and the unique value you bring?

Collect Positive Feedback

Connect with 5-7 people you trust and ask them to share what they believe are your greatest strengths and contributions. Consider connecting with a few people beyond your family and friends. Collect their responses and look for common thoughts, opinions, and surprising insights. External perspectives can often reveal the value you may overlook in yourself.

1. _____

2. _____

3. _____

4. _____

5. _____
   _____
   _____
   _____
   _____

6. _____
   _____
   _____
   _____
   _____

7. _____
   _____
   _____
   _____

Collect More Positive Feedback

Hey Global Girl,
Partner with God to accomplish your purpose.

Here is space to write, create, or do both.

Date: ___ / ___ / ___

Date: ___ / ___ / ___

Embracing Purpose

Discovering your purpose is like finding a compass when you are lost in the woods. Once you understand and embrace your purpose, it guides your life journey, couples your passions with strategic actions, and leads you toward a life of fulfillment and extraordinary impact.

Embracing your God-given purpose will allow you to take control of your life, and become the person you were always meant to be. It will lead you to creative ways to show up in the world as you shape a life lived in and on purpose.

Identifying Your Purpose

Do the thing that sets your soul on fire for God and makes you come alive.

Maybe you are a natural-born encourager, someone who always lifts others up with your words. Perhaps you have a knack for teaching, breaking down complex concepts into easily digestible concepts. Or, maybe you have the ability to influence people and they come to you for your ideas and directions on matters that concern them. Whatever your IT is, do not hide it. Let it shine!

For me, I come alive when I am facilitating a workshop or teaching in a classroom setting. No matter what I am discussing or teaching, in those moments, I feel God whenever I am in those spaces, whether in person or virtually. It is really a euphoric experience. And, the feedback I receive from participants reflects their satisfaction in ways that let me know that what I felt inwardly was pouring out into the space. Those moments let me know that I was created to teach. While that has evolved over time, from high school, University lecture halls, and professional workshops, to online education, I am still a teacher at my core. It is one of the threads that is woven into what I embrace as my God-given purpose.

So, what lights your flame and sets your identity on fire? Whatever your answer is, I encourage you to embrace your purpose as the Apostle Paul says, in Romans 12:6-8,

We have different gifts, according to the grace given to each of us. If your gift is prophesying, then prophesy in accordance with your faith; if it is serving, then serve; if it is teaching, then teach; if it is to encourage, then give encouragement; if it is giving, then give generously; if it is to lead, do it diligently; if it is to show mercy, do it cheerfully.

Simply put, the Apostle Paul lets us know that we are unique and there is something within each of us that is waiting to shine. Your IT is waiting to burst forth and illuminate the world around you. So, let your light shine. Come alive.

Lord,

Today, I come to You as humbly as I know how not asking but thanking You for the unique talents and gifts You placed down on the inside of me. Thank You for helping me recognize and embrace every talent, skill, and ability. Help me use them to let Your light shine that people might see Your good works in me. Father, I thank You for allowing me to identify that thing that You would like me to explore, embrace, and cultivate. I thank You for illuminating the divine purpose You want me to accomplish. May my life be a reflection of Your goodness and grace, be a light in darkness, and bring hope to those in need.

In Jesus' mighty name. Amen.

Embracing Purpose Study Scriptures

May these scriptures lead you to embrace or further explore your purpose. Read, study, or meditate on them day, night, or anytime in between.

Keep this Book of the Law always on your lips; meditate on it day and night, so that you may be careful to do everything written in it. Then you will be prosperous and successful. (Joshua 1:8)

Let your light so shine before men, that they may see your good works, and glorify your Father which is in heaven. (Matthew 5:16)

Date: ___ / ___ / ___

Write a letter to your future self and share advice for reaching your God-given purpose. Be sure to tell your future self why you are necessary, valuable, and uniquely made to do what God placed down on the inside of you.

Dear _____,

_____
_____
_____
_____
_____
_____
_____
_____
_____
_____
_____
_____
_____
_____
_____
_____
_____
_____
_____
_____
_____
_____
_____

Date: ___ / ___ / ___

When you think about your future, what do you see yourself doing in the next five to ten years when it comes to stepping into your purpose? Be sure to be as detailed as possible. Explain how and why you see yourself getting there.

Date: ___ / ___ / ___

It is time to be intentional about your purpose! Create a list of intentions that will support your forward progress toward living fully in your purpose. Set your intentions and live by them.

"I intend to seek God regularly through prayer and fasting about my purpose."

"I intend to continuously explore the depths of my purpose."

"I intend to acquire the necessary training to help flourish in my purpose."

"I intend to live a life of purpose with authenticity."

_____

_____

_____

_____

_____

_____

_____

_____

_____

_____

_____

_____

_____

_____

_____

_____

Daily Affirmations for Embracing Your Purpose

Write seven positive affirmations for embracing your purpose. Recite them in the mirror daily, until your thoughts, feelings, and emotions align with your words.

"I will make good decisions daily."

"I live a life of meaning."

1. _____
   _____

2. _____
   _____

3. _____
   _____

4. _____
   _____

5. _____
   _____

6. _____
   _____

7. _____
   _____

Hey Global Girl,
Embrace your multi-layered life with
faith, know-how, and grit.

Here is space to write, create, or do both.

Date: ___ / ___ / ___

Date: ___ / ___ / ___

Frame the life you want
to live with your words.
Write the vision.
Then, speak it.

Living Out Your Vision & Mission

I started mastering the art of leading with my priorities. I think I started doing it unconsciously. Then, it hit me in a conversation with a colleague; I am super intentional about doing things I know serve my God-given purpose. Anything outside of my priorities just sits in my personal parking lot until it becomes important enough to address. Though I know that may sound a little harsh to some, I live by the notion that there is too much at stake not to obey God concerning His strategy and plans for life. So, when God gives me instruction or an idea, I am laser focused on what He has asked of me. Because one thing I know for sure is that if God said it, it is going to work. Like Proverbs 19:21 says, *"Many are the plans in a person's heart, but it is the Lord's purpose that prevails."*

So yes, I am intentional about every task or idea I seek to conquer. And because I know the Lord's plan for me is big, it requires such intentional focus and effort that I literally do not have time to waste. In my youth, God gave me a glimpse of my future. Therefore, I have committed my life to fulfilling His purpose in everything I do, of course, with a little balance and time to refuel.

That is why one of the Scriptures I live by is Habakkuk 2:2-3 (New King James),

"Then the Lord answered me and said: "Write the vision And make it plain on tablets, That he may run who reads it. For the vision is yet for an appointed time; But at the end it will speak, and it will not lie. Though it tarries, wait for it; Because it will surely come, It will not tarry . . . ."

I love the revelation in this Scripture. Here, Habakkuk explains that if you write your vision clearly where you can read and study it, it will help you stay focused. No matter what is going on all around you, writing it down will remind you what God said about you. Therefore, you will be able to run with it. Or, in other words, because vision is futuristic and often much bigger and bolder than you can handle in your present circumstance or ability, you must learn to embrace, understand, study, and train for it. Our collective goal must be to prepare our future selves to step fully into purpose when it is our appointed time.

So, *Global Girl*, will you lean into Habakkuk 2:2-3? Will you be ready at your appointed time?

Dear Heavenly Father,

Only You know my end from my beginning. Father, it is through You that I will be able to understand the plans and path You have for my life. Thank You, Father, for opening my eyes to Your vision and mission for my life. Thank You for aligning my desires with Your will for my life.

Lord, as I embrace my purpose, give me the confidence to embrace everything You reveal to me about my future and destiny. Point me toward the divine connections that will help me answer the calling that I feel from within. Send the right resources to help me fulfill everything You desire for me to do. Help me to trust in Your timing, even when it feels like I am running out of time. Give me patience as I wait for Your revelation, and fill me with hope as I eagerly anticipate the amazing things You have in store.

Lord, help me to number my days and make good use of the time You have given me to learn and grow toward the vision, mission, and purpose for my life.

In Jesus' name I pray. Amen.

Embracing Purpose Study Scriptures

May these scriptures lead you to embrace or further explore your purpose. Read, study, or meditate on them day, night, or anytime in between.

For I know the plans I have for you," declares the Lord, "plans to prosper you and not to harm you, plans to give you hope and a future. (Jeremiah 29:11)

"You did not choose me, but I chose you and appointed you that you should go and bear fruit and that your fruit should abide, so that whatever you ask the Father in my name, he may give it to you." (John 15:16)

Date: ___ / ___ / ___

What do you believe the Lord is saying to you about your personal vision and mission for your life? In what ways have you received confirmation or guidance from the Lord about it?

Write the Vision

Create a personal vision statement that describes what you want to achieve in the next five to ten years.

"I will expand Girl Go Global™ into a worldwide missions organization that supports women and girls. I will use my best gifts, skills, and talents to spread the gospel of Jesus. In doing so, I will be feeding my soul and fulfilling my purpose. I will offer business, professional, and life skills development training. I will also provide resources to help support their basic needs like food, clothes, and shelter."
- Dr. Jasmine Leigh Morse

My personal vision statement.

_____

_____

_____

_____

_____

_____

_____

_____

_____

_____

_____

_____

_____

Write the Mission

Create a brief personal mission statement that defines who you are and what you want to achieve. A good personal mission statement will help support your personal long-term vision statement.

"To inspire and empower women to embrace their multi-layered lives with faith, know-how, and grit."
- Dr. Jasmine Leigh Morse

My personal mission statement.

_____
_____
_____
_____
_____
_____
_____
_____
_____
_____
_____
_____
_____

Connect to your vision and mission by creating a vision board here.

Hey Global Girl,
Your appointed time to flourish in your purpose is on the way. Write the vision.

Here is space to write, create, or do both.

Date: ___ / ___ / ___

Date: ___ / ___ / ___

I am excited about my future. God, you promised me good success. I join my faith + my works to reach my goals.

Setting Purpose-Filled Goals

Brothers and sisters, I do not consider myself yet to have taken hold of it. But one thing I do: Forgetting what is behind and straining toward what is ahead, I press on toward the goal to win the prize for which God has called me heavenward in Christ Jesus. (Philippians 3:13-14)

Goals are just that . . . goals. They are the thing you set out to accomplish not knowing what the true outcome will be. Goals are also the intention many of us have learned to outline before we set out to fulfill our short or long-term ideas.

Despite how exciting it can be for some of us to sit down and write down our goals for the next 5-10 years, too often, setting goals can be intimidating. For some, goal setting leads to overwhelming emotions because of the unknown outcome, uncertainty of skills, financial resources needed, time, procrastination, and so much more. For many others, goal setting also invokes feelings of fear, coupled with the question, "Can I actually do this?"

Yet, no matter what goal I set, I believe what Jesus says, in Luke 18, *"What is impossible with man is possible with God."* And I encourage you to do the same with confidence and courage. You see, God knows the desires of our hearts, and He wants us to succeed. He is not sitting back waiting for us to figure it out on our own. He is right there beside us, cheering us on every step of the way.

So, if you are feeling overwhelmed or discouraged, remember that God's got your back. His timing is always perfect, and He is never late. He is always on time.

Heavenly Father,

Thank You for this day. Thank You for another opportunity to come before You in prayer. It is through Your kindness and love for me that You give me the clarity I need to understand why and for what purpose I was born. Lord, it is through You that I have a purpose on Earth. It is through You that I can understand the direction and strategies You have for me now and in the future. Lord, grant me the wisdom to understand which goals I should pursue. Give me the when, where, and how for my future. Give me the clarity of thought to make wise decisions as I continue to seek You for direction in my life.

In Jesus' name. Amen.

Embracing Purpose Study Scriptures

May these scriptures lead you to embrace or further explore your purpose. Read, study, or meditate on them day, night, or anytime in between.

"I am the Lord, the God of all mankind. Is anything too hard for me? . . ."
(Jeremiah 32:27)

I can do all this through him who gives me strength. (Philippians 4:13)

Date: ___ / ___ / ___

What are three big goals that would move you closer to your life vision? What steps can you take in the next six months to start achieving them?

Date: ___ / ___ / ___

Describe your ideal future. Think about your career, professional development, personal growth, and relationships over the next 5-10 years.

Date: ___ / ___ / ___

What is your purpose? Explain the importance of setting goals that align with your purpose and how your goals align with your values and strengths.

_____
_____
_____
_____
_____
_____
_____
_____
_____
_____
_____
_____
_____
_____
_____
_____
_____
_____
_____
_____
_____
_____
_____
_____

Your Purpose & Your Value Proposition

As you begin to think about your purpose, it is important to consider who you will be serving and supporting when it comes to fulfilling your purpose. It is also important to understand the value you wish to add to someone's life. Likewise, your purpose will most often be the answer to someone else's problem.

Purpose: To have clarity regarding why you were created.

What is your purpose?

_____
_____
_____
_____

What problem will your purpose address in someone else's life?

_____
_____
_____
_____

Value Proposition: A simple statement that aligns with your target audience's needs. The core elements of your value proposition should include the relevance and benefits you are bringing to your target audience.

When you think about your purpose, list the top three problems you plan to solve for others? When you live out your purpose, you become the solution to someone's problem.

Solution #1

_____
_____
_____

Solution #2

_____
_____
_____

Solution #3

_____
_____
_____

Now, let's take those three solutions and create your value proposition.

I help [insert target audience] [insert action verb] [insert solution #1], [insert solution #2], and [insert solution #3].

Example: I help [women ages 30-50] (1) _identify_ their zone of genius, (2) _focus_ on their purpose, and (3) _set_ realistic goals.

I help _____ _____
_____ , _____
_____ , and _____
_____.

Hey Global Girl,
There is nothing impossible with God.

Here is space to write, create, or do both.

Date: ___ / ___ / ___

Date: ___ / ___ / ___

Igniting Purpose

Unleash your strengths, passions, values, and a version of yourself that the world and community around you need. When you activate your purpose, you will not only light up your path, but you will also light the way for others who need to find their path to purpose.

Invite God into your plans.

Creating a Purpose-Filled Plan

Are you a to-do list girl, or do you just go with the flow? Do you plan your days, months, and years, or do you prefer some planning with the hope that everything else will fall into place? Wherever you find yourself, Proverbs 16:3 gives us a gentle nudge to invite God into our planning sessions, as it says, *"Commit to the Lord whatever you do, and he will establish your plans."* I know I am not the only one who gets caught up in what may be good ideas. But, what is important to me is ensuring that I am putting my action and effort behind God's ideas for my life.

So, as you continue to map out your goals, hopes, and dreams, take a moment to pause and invite God into your plans. He is not just interested in the big stuff. He cares about every detail of your life. When you commit your plans to Him, He promises to guide you and establish your plans according to His perfect will.

Dear Heavenly Father,

Forgive me if I have tried to walk in my own way. Create in me a clean heart and renew in me a right spirit. Cast me not away from thy presence. Please do not take Your Holy Spirit from me. Restore in me the joy of salvation so that I may honor You with all my heart, soul, mind, body, and actions. Lord, thank You for trusting me with purpose. Thank You for igniting Your purpose in my heart. Thank You for creating me to create something for Your glory. Father, I commit my plans to You and align my plans with Your will for my life. Help me surrender my flesh unto You. Give me a river of righteousness that allows me to operate in my purpose with clean hands and a pure heart.

In Jesus' name. Amen.

Igniting Purpose Study Scriptures

May these scriptures lead you to ignite or further explore your purpose. Read, study, or meditate on them day, night, or anytime in between.

We can make our own plans, but the Lord gives the right answer. People may be pure in their own eyes, but the Lord examines their motives. Commit your actions to the Lord, and your plans will succeed. (Proverbs 16:1-4)

May the God of hope fill you with all joy and peace as you trust in him, so that you may overflow with hope by the power of the Holy Spirit. (Romans 15:13)

Date: ___ / ___ / ___

Reflect on the importance of seeking God's guidance and wisdom to create your purpose-filled plans.

Date: ___ / ___ / ___

Imagine the goals you need to set in order to operate in your purpose. What daily habits or routines would contribute to your success? What would an average day in your life look like?

Date: ___ / ___ / ___

Reflect on your challenges and victories from the past three to five years. What lessons learned can you take with you into your future?

Create a Word Map

Create a Word Map that represents your goals. Include words and phrases that inspire and motivate you. Write a brief reflection on how your word map aligns with your vision, mission, and goals.

Purpose

List Your Goals

Make a list of your top short-term and long-term goals associated with your purpose.

Short-Terms Goals (At least 3 months to 2 years)	**Long-Term Goals** (3-5 years or more)

*Hey Global Girl,
Make plans to step into your purpose.
Learn and grow from challenges, and
celebrate your successes.*

Here is space to write, create, or do both.

Date: ___ / ___ / ___

Date: ___ / ___ / ___

I thrive in purpose with boldness.

Tracking the Success of Your Purpose-Filled Plan

As you set out to pursue destiny and purpose, always remember the God of everything and everywhere. Never let the busyness of life overtake you so much that you do not build an infrastructure that includes God.

With all this talk about artificial intelligence (AI) and automation in the world right now, I have been thinking about a few things, especially as I begin to further infuse automation into my business and day-to-day activities. So, hear me out . . . I was wondering . . .

Is my relationship with God running on autopilot? Does my relationship with my Heavenly Father have a workflow in place to help me navigate life more effectively?

When I face a challenge, do I have a system in place that automatically sets up a meeting with my Chief Strategist, Christ the King of Kings?

I have been so intentional about understanding my business' automated workflows and client management system. I even have monthly subscription services: dry cleaning pickup, weekly meal prep delivery, specialty laundry detergent, business networking groups, and more. So, I was wondering whether I have been this focused on my relationship with Jesus Christ.

Just as I have established business workflows and automations that help me navigate life more efficiently, I want my relationship with Christ to have a system and rhythm that allows my most important relationship to run on autopilot. I want it to have a rhythm that helps me operate no matter what circumstance I face. Just like AI tools run on autopilot by generating content, sending emails, or scheduling meetings, I want my response to the cares of life to automatically cause me to lift my hands in praise and thanksgiving. I want my automatic response to be that I fall on my knees in prayer or search the Scriptures for the answers I need. I want my relationship with Christ to have a flow.

In a culture that consistently changes, I want to have a profound desire to stay connected to my source, Jesus Christ. Just like I strive to automate my daily tasks, I believe I can automate my relationship with the Lord. And let me be clear, I do not want my relationship to be prescriptive or mundane. I want my relationship to be personalized and ever-evolving so much so that my system and my automatic response with the Lord has room to expand like a funnel that starts out with 10 subscribers and grows to hundreds of thousands over time.

Like seriously, God really gave us the blueprint and ultimate workflow for building our lives with Him right in His Word! Scripture says, in Psalms 119:105 *"Your word is a lamp for my feet, a light on my path."*

Can you imagine—a seamless flow where devotion becomes a part of our every breath? One where your day starts and ends with thoughts about the goodness of Jesus. One where each day starts and ends with a prayer and Scripture reading. One where your deeds are like hymns to the Father and your thoughts are like silent conversations with God. One where you see God in good and difficult experiences.

Can you imagine your relationship with Christ lived out loud so much so that *". . . the words of [your] mouth, and the meditation of [your] heart, be acceptable in thy sight, O Lord, [your] strength, and [your] redeemer"* (Psalm 19:14 KJV)?

In the realm of technology, we set reminders to ensure we do not forget crucial tasks. Likewise, I encourage you to set a reminder to pray in the middle of your day or take 15 minutes to read and meditate on a Scripture. As you seek more of God concerning your purpose, practice further infusing God into your workflow for life ... your routine, and do not let anything distract you. Your purpose depends on it.

> ### *Lord,*
>
> I want to build a system and workflow that includes You. Teach me to handle the purpose You have for me with balance and boundaries. Teach me to number my day so that my life will be purpose-filled and focused. Help me to trust in Your guidance, even when everything around me seems uncertain. Give me the strength and courage to embrace the changes and transitions in my life, knowing that You are with me every step of the way. Thank You for Your faithfulness and for always being a steady anchor in the midst of challenges.
>
> *In Jesus' name I pray. Amen.*

Igniting Purpose Study Scriptures

May these scriptures lead you to ignite or further explore your purpose. Read, study, or meditate on them day, night, or anytime in between.

Don't be afraid, for I am with you. Don't be discouraged, for I am your God. I will strengthen you and help you. I will hold you up with my victorious right hand. (Isaiah 41:10)

For God has not given us a spirit of fear and timidity, but of power, love, and self-discipline. (2 Timothy 1:7)

Date: ___ / ___ / ___

What are five goals that would move you closer to your life purpose? What steps can you take in the next six months to start achieving them?

Date: ___ / ___ / ___

As a follower of Jesus Christ, in what ways can you ensure your goals reflect the attributes of God?

Date: ___ / ___ / ___

How can you involve God in your purpose-planning process and seek His guidance?

Create a Purpose Action Plan

Develop a timeline for achieving your goals. Include key action items and deadlines for each goal. Reflect on how this timeline helps you stay on track.

Purpose:

_____
_____
_____
_____
_____
_____
_____
_____

Purpose Value Proposition:

_____
_____
_____
_____
_____
_____
_____
_____

Goals	Action Items Associated with Each Goal	Deadline to Achieve Action Items
Goal #1		
Goal #2		
Goal #3		
Goal #4		
Goal #5		

Resources Needed	Potential Barriers/ Challenges	Status/Outcome

Hey Global Girl,
Explore and evolve with your purpose.

Here is space to write, create, or do both.

Date: ___ / ___ / ___

Date: ___ / ___ / ___

Prepare for the future you desire. Be intentional, focused, and strategic.

Re-evaluating Your Ever-Evolving Purpose-Filled Plan

This section is dedicated to your continuous exploration and evolution. Write your prayers, continue to study scriptures, refine your goals, and more. There is also open space for you to write, create, or do both.

Daily Affirmations for Discovering, Embracing, and Igniting Purpose

Write seven purpose affirmations to help you continue your journey. Recite them daily until your thoughts, feelings, and emotions align with your words.

"I wait patiently on the promises of God."

1. _____
_____

2. _____
_____

3. _____
_____

4. _____
_____

5. _____
_____

6. _____
_____

7. _____
_____

Igniting Purpose Study Scriptures

Use this space to highlight study Scriptures that speak to where you are on your purpose journey. May these Scriptures lead you to embrace or further explore your purpose.

Your Purpose Prayer

Write a daily prayer for reaching your purpose and destiny. Consider praying for your relationship with God, resources, divine connections, financial stability, and so much more. Be specific!

Date: ___ / ___ / ___

In what ways will fulfilling your purpose add value to your life?

Hey Global Girl,
Continuous evaluation and adaptation is one of the currencies of progress.

Here is space to write, create, or do both.

Date: ___ / ___ / ___

Date: ___ / ___ / ___

Date: ___ / ___ / ___

Hey Global Girl,

Let's go global girl and embrace our multi-layered lives.

XOXO,

Dr. Jasmine

Purpose Notes

Date: ___ / ___ / ___

Date: ___ / ___ / ___

Date: ___ / ___ / ___

Date: ___ / ___ / ___

Date: ___ / ___ / ___

Date: ___ / ___ / ___

Date: ___ / ___ / ___

Date: ___ / ___ / ___

Date: ___ / ___ / ___

Date: ___ / ___ / ___

Date: ___ / ___ / ___

Date: ___ / ___ / ___

Date: ___ / ___ / ___

Date: ___ / ___ / ___

Date: ___ / ___ / ___

Date: __ / __ / __

Date: ___ / ___ / ___

Date: ___ / ___ / ___

Date: ___ / ___ / ___

Date: ___ / ___ / ___

Date: ___ / ___ / ___

Date: ___ / ___ / ___

Date: ___ / ___ / ___

Date: ___ / ___ / ___

Date: ___ / ___ / ___

Date: ___ / ___ / ___

Date: ___ / ___ / ___

Date: ___ / ___ / ___

Date: ___ / ___ / ___

Date: ___ / ___ / ___

Date: ___ / ___ / ___

Date: ___ / ___ / ___

Date: ___ / ___ / ___

Date: ___ / ___ / ___

Date: ___ / ___ / ___

Date: ___ / ___ / ___

Date: ___ / ___ / ___

Date: ___ / ___ / ___

Date: ___ / ___ / ___

Date: ___ / ___ / ___

Date: ___ / ___ / ___

Date: ___ / ___ / ___

Date: ___ / ___ / ___

Date: ___ / ___ / ___

Date: ___ / ___ / ___

Date: ___ / ___ / ___

Date: ___ / ___ / ___

Date: ___ / ___ / ___

Date: ___ / ___ / ___

Date: ___ / ___ / ___

Date: ___ / ___ / ___

Date: ___ / ___ / ___

About The Author

Dr. Jasmine Leigh Morse is a multi-talented author, educator, entrepreneur, and founder of *Girl Go Global*™, a community for purpose-driven women. For 20+ years, Dr. Jasmine has used her unique skills as an educator, professional writer, and communications strategist to build a career that allows her to serve small business owners, in academia, and at all levels of government. Whether she is mentoring women and girls, engaging students during university lectures, speaking as keynote, or serving at all levels of government, she is driven by providing support to others to meet needs, equip, and train. In addition to making the Daily Record's Successful by 40 Very Important Professionals list, she is a President's Management Council Fellow and writer with interests in topics that concern women.

Visit www.girlgoglobal.com to learn more about the online community for purpose-driven women.

Other Books By Dr. Jasmine

Heart Rhythms: Surviving Singleness with Faith, Know-How, and Grit

Heart Rhythms: A Guided Journal for Thriving in Singleness

www.ingramcontent.com/pod-product-compliance
Lightning Source LLC
Chambersburg PA
CBHW072156070526
44585CB00015B/1166